KINGSFORD®

GREAT BARBECUES

Publications International, Ltd.

Recipe Development: Suzanne Carreiro, Dorothy Nicholson

Photography: Sacco Productions Limited, Chicago
Photographer: Marc A. Frisco
Photo Stylist: Melissa J. Frisco
Production: Paula M. Walters
Food Stylists: Kim Hartman, Teri Rys-Maki
Assistant Food Stylist: Susie Skoog

Pictured on the front cover: Classic Grilled Chicken *(page 16)*.
Pictured on the back cover *(top to bottom):* Mediterranean Grilled Vegetables *(page 66)*, Grilled Paella *(page 30)*, Pork Chop with Apple-Sage Stuffing *(page 22)* and Pesto Chicken and Pepper Wrap *(page 82)*.

ISBN: 0-7853-2237-X

Manufactured in U.S.A.

8 7 6 5 4 3 2 1

Nutritional Analysis: Nutritional information is given for the recipes in this publication. Each analysis is based on the food items in the ingredient list, except ingredients labeled as "optional" or "for garnish." When more than one ingredient choice is listed, the first ingredient is used for analysis. If a range for the amount of an ingredient is given, the nutritional analysis is based on the lowest amount. Foods offered as "serve with" suggestions are not included in the analysis unless otherwise stated.

KINGSFORD

GREAT BARBECUES

Barbecue Basics

A DASH OF HISTORY

Henry Ford deserved credit for more than the Model T. His ingenuity helped create America's passion for outdoor cooking. In the early 1900's, Ford operated a northern Michigan sawmill that made wooden framing for his Model T's. As piles of wood scraps grew, he searched for a way to make them useful. He soon learned how to chip the wood and convert it into the now familiar pillow-shaped briquets. These convenient briquets, originally sold through Ford automobile agencies, marked the beginning of the all-American tradition of barbecuing.

Ford Charcoal, later named **Kingsford**® charcoal briquets, is the original and still the No. 1 brand sold in the nation today.

WHAT TYPE OF CHARCOAL?

Successful barbecuing starts with a good fire. Premium quality briquets, such as **Kingsford**® charcoal, help deliver a perfect fire in three ways. They light quicker so the coals are ready sooner. They burn longer to provide more cooking time. They perform consistently, bag after bag.

Match Light® ready-to-light charcoal briquets are especially good for midweek barbecues when time is at a premium. They already contain just the right amount of lighter fluid to produce a quick-starting fire. Simply stack the briquets into a pyramid and light several briquets with a match. The coals will be ready in about 15 minutes. Be sure to close the bag tightly after each use.

A single-use lightable bag of charcoal, such as **BBQ Bag**®, is the convenient choice for tailgate parties or other away-from-home grilling. Just light the bag, which is filled with enough ready-to-light briquets for one barbecue.

Kingsford® **with Mesquite** charcoal briquets are a blend of compressed charcoal briquets and mesquite chips. They produce mesquite smoke to enhance the flavor of outdoor fare without the risk of uneven burning and hotter temperatures associated with pure mesquite charcoal.

Since charcoal is porous and will absorb moisture, always store it in a dry area and keep the bag in a tightly closed container. Charcoal that has been exposed to humidity or moisture can be more difficult to light.

SAFETY FIRST

The grill should be stable and set away from shrubbery, grass and overhangs. Make sure grill vents are not clogged with ashes before starting a fire. NEVER use gasoline or kerosene as a lighter fluid. Either one can cause an explosion. To get a sluggish fire going, do not add lighter fluid directly to hot coals. Instead, place 4 or 5 new briquets in a metal can and add lighter fluid. With long-handled tongs, add new briquets to the pyramid of briquets, then light with a match. These new briquets will restart the fire.

Remember that coals are hot (up to 1000°F) and that the heat transfers to the barbecue grill, grid, tools and food. Always wear heavy-duty mitts when cooking and handling the grill and tools.

BUILDING PERFECT FIRES

How Much Charcoal? A 5-pound bag of **Kingsford**® charcoal contains 90 to 100 briquets, a 10-pound bag between 180 to 200, and a 20-pound bag 360 to 400 briquets. The number of briquets required for barbecuing depends on the size and type of grill and the amount of food to be prepared. Weather conditions also have an effect; strong winds, very cold temperatures or very humid conditions increase the number of briquets needed for a good fire. As a rule, it takes about 30 briquets to grill 1 pound of meat.

For **direct cooking,** food is placed directly over the coals. Make sure there is enough charcoal in a single layer to extend 1 to 2 inches beyond the area of the food. Pour briquets into the grill to determine the quantity needed, then stack into a pyramid.

For **indirect cooking,** food is placed over a drip pan and the coals are banked either to one side or on both sides of the pan. This method is recommended for large cuts of meat, such as roasts and fatty meats, to eliminate flame flare-ups. Here's how to determine the number of briquets needed:

BRIQUETS NEEDED FOR INDIRECT COOKING IN A COVERED GRILL

Briquets needed on each side of drip pan for cooking 45 to 50 minutes

Diameter of Grill (inches)	Number of Briquets
26¾	30
22½	25
18½	16
14	15

Briquets needed to be added on each side of drip pan every 45 minutes— use only regular briquets

Diameter of Grill (inches)	Number of Briquets
26¾	9
22½	8
18½	5
14	4

Using Lighter Fluid: Kingsford® Odorless charcoal lighter is formulated to meet strict air-quality standards. Stack briquets into a pyramid. Use about ¼ cup of fluid per pound of briquets (18 to 20), then light with a match. Coals will be ready in about 20 minutes, when they are about 70% ashed over. At night, they will have a noticeable reddish glow.

Using a Chimney Starter: This method is essentially failure-proof. No lighter fluid is required. Remove the grid and set the starter in the base of the grill. Crumple a few sheets of newspaper and place them in the bottom of the starter. Fill the top portion with charcoal briquets. Light the newspaper. Do not disturb the starter; coals will be ready in about 20 minutes. Wear fireproof mitts when lifting the starter.

Using an Electric Starter: Nestle the electric starter in the briquets. Plug it into a heavy-duty extension cord, then plug the cord into an outlet. After 8 to 10 minutes, when ash begins to form on the briquets, unplug the starter, remove it, and carefully set it aside. Arrange the briquets in a single layer, close together.

How Hot is the Grill? If you don't have a grill thermometer, estimate the temperature on the grill surface by holding your hand, palm side down, just above the grid. Count "one thousand one, one thousand two," etc., until the heat is uncomfortable. If you can keep your hand in place:

2 seconds—hot fire, 375°F or more.
3 seconds—medium-hot fire, 350° to 375°F.
4 seconds—medium fire, 300° to 350°F.
5 seconds—low fire, 200° to 300°F.

FLAVORED SMOKE

Flavored smoke, a combination of heady aromas from hardwoods and fresh or dried herbs, imparts a special flavor to barbecued foods. As a rule, a little goes a long way. Added flavorings should complement, not overpower, food's natural taste. Always soak flavorings, such as wood chunks, wood chips or herbs, in water at least 30 minutes before adding to coals. The flavorings should smolder and smoke, not burn.

Hickory and mesquite chips or wood chunks are the most readily available flavorings. Look for **Kingsford®** Hickory and **Kingsford®** Mesquite wood chips in your store's barbecue section.

Small bunches of fresh or dried herbs soaked in water can add fragrant flavor as well. Rosemary, oregano and tarragon, for example, can be teamed with wood chips or simply used by themselves for a new taste twist.

TOOLS AND ACCESSORIES

These tools will help make your barbecuing safer and more convenient.

Long-Handled Tongs, Basting Brush and Spatula: Moving hot coals and food around the grill, as well as basting and turning foods, can be dangerous. Select tools with long handles and hang them where you are working. You may want to purchase two pairs of tongs—one for coals and one for food.

Meat Thermometer: The best way to judge the doneness of meat is with a high-quality meat thermometer. Always remember to insert the thermometer into the center of the largest muscle of the meat, with the point away from bone, fat or rotisserie rod.

Heavy-Duty Mitts: You will prevent burns by safeguarding your hands with big, thick mitts. Keep them close to the grill so they are always handy.

Aluminum Foil Drip Pans: A drip pan placed beneath grilling meats will prevent flare-ups. The pan should be $1\frac{1}{2}$ inches deep and extend about 3 inches beyond the ends of the meat. The juices that collect in the drip pan may be used for a sauce or gravy. Bring drippings to a boil before using.

Water Spritzer: To quench flare-ups, use a water-filled spray bottle.

Other Tools and Accessories: A charcoal chimney or electric charcoal starter is useful for starting the fire without lighter fluid. Hinged wire baskets facilitate the turning of some foods, such as fish fillets. Long skewers made of metal or wood are indispensable for kabobs. Wooden skewers should be soaked in water at least 20 minutes before grilling to prevent the wood from burning.

DRY RUBS AND MARINADES

Dry rubs of seasonings and spices are rubbed onto meat for flavor before grilling. They include ground black or white pepper, paprika and garlic powder. Some also include mustard, brown sugar and cayenne pepper. Crushed herbs, such as sage, basil and thyme, are other good choices.

Marinades add flavor, but they also help tenderize less tender cuts of meat. Marinades include an acidic ingredient for tenderizing, such as wine, vinegar or lemon juice, combined with herbs, seasonings and oil. Fish and vegetables don't need tenderizing and should be marinated for only 15 to 30 minutes.

Meat and poultry should be marinated for a few hours or as long as overnight. Turn marinating foods occasionally to let the flavor infuse evenly. For safety, marinate all meats, poultry and seafood in the refrigerator. Resealable plastic food storage bags are great to hold foods as they marinate.

Reserve some of the marinade before adding the meat, poultry or seafood. Use this reserved marinade as a baste while the meat is cooking. You can also serve marinade that has been drained from the meat as a dipping sauce. However, follow food safety practices; place marinade in a saucepan and bring to a full boil for at least 1 minute. This is necessary to prevent the cooked food from becoming contaminated with bacteria that may be present in the marinade from the raw meat, poultry or seafood.

A WORD ABOUT SAUCES

Sauces add delicious flavors to almost any grilled fare. Premium sauces, such as K.C. Masterpiece® Barbecue Sauce, capture real homemade taste and are a barbecue staple worth using often. Serve warmed sauce on the side for some added zest. To protect the rich, deep color and spicy flavor of barbecue sauce from burning, baste:

Steaks and chops during the last 3 minutes of grilling.

Chicken during the last 10 minutes of grilling, turning once.

Hot dogs and sausage during the last 5 to 6 minutes.

Barbecued meats (cooked by indirect heat) during the last hour of cooking.

Smoked meats during the last 30 to 45 minutes.

Classics

Baby Back Ribs

¼ cup packed brown sugar
2 tablespoons dry mustard
2 teaspoons paprika
2 teaspoons salt
1 teaspoon black pepper

2 racks pork baby back ribs
   (3½ to 4 pounds)
⅓ to ½ cup K.C. Masterpiece
   Original Barbecue Sauce

Combine sugar, mustard, paprika, salt and pepper. Rub mixture evenly onto ribs to coat. Place ribs on covered grill opposite medium Kingsford briquets. Grill 30 to 45 minutes or until tender and cooked through, turning once and brushing with barbecue sauce during last 10 minutes of grilling.   *Makes 4 servings*

Nutrients per Serving: Calories: 421, protein: 39 g, fat: 21 g, carbohydrate: 17 g, sodium: 1451 mg, cholesterol: 62 mg

Garlic-Dijon Butterflied Lamb

½ cup red wine vinegar
¼ cup coarse-grained mustard
8 cloves garlic, minced
2 tablespoons minced fresh
   rosemary

1 tablespoon olive oil
½ teaspoon salt
½ teaspoon black pepper
4 pounds butterflied boneless
   leg of lamb

Combine vinegar, mustard, garlic, rosemary, oil, salt and pepper in large glass dish. Add lamb; turn to coat. Cover and refrigerate at least 8 hours or up to 2 days, turning occasionally. Remove lamb from marinade; discard marinade. Grill lamb on covered grill over medium Kingsford briquets about 25 to 30 minutes until thickest portion is medium-rare or to desired doneness, turning 4 times.   *Makes 8 to 10 servings*

Nutrients per Serving (¹⁄₁₀ of Garlic-Dijon Butterflied Lamb): Calories: 333, protein: 48 g, fat: 14 g, carbohydrate: 1 g, sodium: 209 mg, cholesterol: 152 mg

Baby Back Ribs

Tandoori-Style Seafood Kabobs

In India, meat and poultry are cooked in an extremely
hot tandoori clay oven. This method cooks food quickly,
charring the outside and leaving the inside moist. Here, seafood
kabobs are grilled over a medium-hot grill for a similar effect.

½ pound *each* salmon fillet,
 tuna steak and swordfish
 steak*
1 teaspoon salt
1 teaspoon ground cumin
¼ teaspoon black pepper
 Dash ground cinnamon
 Dash ground cloves
 Dash ground nutmeg
 Dash ground cardamom
 (optional)
½ cup plain low-fat yogurt
¼ cup lemon juice

1 piece (1-inch cube) peeled
 fresh ginger, minced
1 tablespoon olive oil
2 cloves garlic, minced
½ jalapeño pepper, seeded
 and minced
½ pound large shrimp, shelled
 with tails intact, deveined
1 *each* red and green bell
 pepper, cut into bite-size
 pieces
 Fresh parsley sprigs
 Fresh chives

Cut fish into 1½-inch cubes; cover and refrigerate. Heat salt and spices in
small skillet over medium heat until fragrant (or spices may be added to
marinade without heating); place spices in 2-quart glass dish. Add yogurt,
lemon juice, ginger, oil, garlic and jalapeño pepper; mix well. Add fish and
shrimp; turn to coat. Cover and refrigerate at least 1 hour but no longer
than 2 hours. Thread a variety of seafood onto each metal or wooden
skewer, alternating with bell peppers. (Soak wooden skewers in hot water
30 minutes to prevent burning.) Grill kabobs over medium-hot Kingsford
briquets about 2 minutes per side until fish flakes easily when tested with
fork and shrimp are pink and opaque. Remove seafood and peppers from
skewers. Garnish with parsley and chives. *Makes 4 servings*

Any firm fish can be substituted for any fish listed above.

Nutrients per Serving: Calories: 278, protein: 40 g, fat: 11 g, carbohydrate: 3 g,
sodium: 271 mg, cholesterol: 101 mg

Tandoori-Style Seafood Kabob

Jamaican Steak

A sweet blend of orange and lime juices, ginger, garlic, and hints of cinnamon and cloves makes the perfect marinade for flank steak.

2 pounds beef flank steak
¼ cup packed brown sugar
3 tablespoons orange juice
3 tablespoons lime juice
3 cloves garlic, minced
1 piece (1½×1 inches) fresh
    ginger, minced
2 teaspoons grated
    orange peel

2 teaspoons grated lime peel
1 teaspoon salt
1 teaspoon black pepper
¼ teaspoon ground cinnamon
⅛ teaspoon ground cloves
    Shredded orange peel
    Shredded lime peel

Score both sides of beef.* Combine sugar, juices, garlic, ginger, grated peels, salt, pepper, cinnamon and cloves in 2-quart glass dish. Add beef; turn to coat. Cover and refrigerate steak at least 2 hours. Remove beef from marinade; discard marinade. Grill beef over medium-hot Kingsford briquets about 6 minutes per side until medium-rare or to desired doneness. Garnish with shredded orange and lime peels.

Makes 6 servings

*To score flank steak, cut ¼-inch-deep diagonal lines about 1 inch apart in surface of steak to form diamond-shaped design.

Nutrients per Serving: Calories: 283, protein: 30 g, fat: 17 g, carbohydrate: 0 g, sodium: 97 mg, cholesterol: 81 mg

Jamaican Steak

Classic Grilled Chicken

Chicken from the grill is a perfect choice for family or friends. Enjoy this classic recipe alone or serve it with Spicy Peanut Sauce (page 18), Cilantro Salsa (page 18) or Italian Salsa Verde (page 19).

1 whole frying chicken*
   (3½ pounds), quartered
¼ cup lemon juice
¼ cup olive oil
2 tablespoons soy sauce

2 large cloves garlic, minced
½ teaspoon sugar
½ teaspoon ground cumin
¼ teaspoon black pepper

Rinse chicken under cold running water; pat dry with paper towels. Arrange chicken in 13×9×2-inch glass baking dish. Combine remaining ingredients in small bowl; pour half of mixture over chicken. Cover and refrigerate chicken at least 1 hour or overnight. Cover and reserve remaining mixture in refrigerator to use for basting. Remove chicken from marinade; discard marinade. Arrange medium Kingsford briquets on each side of large rectangular metal or foil drip pan. Pour hot tap water into drip pan until half full. Place chicken on grid directly above drip pan. Grill chicken, skin side down, on covered grill 25 minutes. Baste with reserved baste. Turn chicken; cook 20 to 25 minutes or until juices run clear and chicken is no longer pink in center. *Makes 6 servings*

Substitute 3½ pounds of chicken parts for whole chicken, if desired. Grill legs and thighs about 35 minutes and breast halves about 25 minutes or until chicken is no longer pink in center, turning once.

Nutrients per Serving (without skin): Calories: 404, protein: 44 g, fat: 24 g, carbohydrate: 1 g, sodium: 255 mg, cholesterol: 137 mg

Classic Grilled Chicken with Italian Salsa Verde (page 19)

Spicy Peanut Sauce

⅔ cup canned coconut milk
4 tablespoons sugar*
2 large cloves garlic, minced
1½ teaspoons minced fresh
  ginger

⅛ teaspoon salt
⅛ to ¼ teaspoon cayenne
  pepper
⅓ cup chunky peanut butter
3 tablespoons lemon juice

Combine coconut milk, sugar, garlic, ginger, salt and pepper in 2-quart saucepan; bring to a boil over high heat. Cook over medium heat 5 minutes, stirring occasionally. Stir in peanut butter and lemon juice; cook and stir 3 minutes. If sauce separates or is too thick, stir in 1 to 2 tablespoons boiling water.

Makes about ¾ cup

If peanut butter contains sugar, decrease sugar to 3 tablespoons.

Nutrients per Serving (3 tablespoons): Calories: 168, protein: 5 g, fat: 15 g, carbohydrate: 6 g, sodium: 115 mg, cholesterol: 0 mg

Cilantro Salsa

2 cups packed cilantro leaves
½ small red onion, coarsely
  chopped
2 tablespoons lemon juice
2 tablespoons water
1 to 2 jalapeño peppers,
  seeded and coarsely
  chopped

¾ teaspoon sugar
½ teaspoon salt
¼ teaspoon black pepper

Combine all ingredients in food processor; process until well blended, scraping sides of bowl several times. Serve at room temperature with grilled chicken, fish, pork or lamb. Refrigerate leftovers.

Makes about 1 cup

Nutrients per Serving (¼ cup): Calories: 15, protein: 0 g, fat: trace, carbohydrate: 3 g, sodium: 271 mg, cholesterol: 0 mg

Italian Salsa Verde

½ cup packed Italian parsley, finely chopped
¼ cup olive oil
3 tablespoons lemon juice

2 tablespoons capers, chopped
1 shallot *or* 2 green onions, thinly sliced
⅛ teaspoon black pepper

Combine all ingredients in small bowl; let stand about 30 minutes. Serve at room temperature with grilled chicken or fish; refrigerate leftovers.

Makes about ⅔ cup

Nutrients per Serving (about 2½ tablespoons): Calories: 128, protein: 0 g, fat: 15 g, carbohydrate: 2 g, sodium: 162 mg, cholesterol: 0 mg

Perfectly Grilled Steak & Potatoes

Olive oil
1½ teaspoons cracked black pepper
2 cloves garlic, pressed
Salt
½ teaspoon dried thyme leaves
4 beef tenderloin steaks or boneless top loin steaks, 1½ inches thick

4 medium potatoes, cut into ½-inch slices
Ground black pepper
Lime wedges

Combine 2 tablespoons oil, cracked pepper, garlic, ½ teaspoon salt and thyme in cup. Brush oil mixture over steaks to coat both sides. Brush potato slices with additional oil; season to taste with additional salt and ground pepper. Lightly oil hot grid to prevent sticking. Grill beef on covered grill over medium-hot Kingsford briquets 10 to 12 minutes for medium-rare or to desired doneness, turning once. Grill potatoes 10 to 12 minutes or until golden brown and tender, turning once. Serve steaks with potatoes and lime wedges.

Makes 4 servings

Nutrients per Serving: Calories: 527, protein: 33 g, fat: 21 g, carbohydrate: 52 g, sodium: 451 mg, cholesterol: 76 mg

Barbecued Salmon

4 salmon steaks,
   ¾ to 1 inch thick
3 tablespoons lemon juice
2 tablespoons soy sauce
   Salt and black pepper

½ cup K.C. Masterpiece
   Original Barbecue Sauce
Fresh oregano sprigs
Grilled mushrooms

Rinse salmon; pat dry with paper towels. Combine lemon juice and soy sauce in shallow glass dish. Add salmon; let stand at cool room temperature no more than 15 to 20 minutes, turning salmon several times. Remove salmon from marinade; discard marinade. Season lightly with salt and pepper.

Lightly oil hot grid to prevent sticking. Grill salmon on covered grill over medium Kingsford briquets 10 to 14 minutes. Halfway through cooking time brush salmon with barbecue sauce, then turn and continue grilling until fish flakes easily when tested with fork. Remove fish from grill; brush with barbecue sauce. Garnish with oregano sprigs and mushrooms.

Makes 4 servings

Nutrients per Serving: Calories: 215, protein: 25 g, fat: 10 g, carbohydrate: 4 g, sodium: 433 mg, cholesterol: 70 mg

Barbecued Salmon

Pork Chops with Apple-Sage Stuffing

The sweetness of apple and the herblike essence of vermouth combine with sage to create a delicious stuffing for pork.

6 center-cut pork chops
(3 pounds), about 1 inch
thick
¾ cup dry vermouth, divided
4 tablespoons minced fresh
sage *or* 4 teaspoons
rubbed sage, divided
2 tablespoons soy sauce
1 tablespoon olive oil
2 cloves garlic, minced

½ teaspoon black pepper,
divided
1 tablespoon butter
1 medium onion, diced
1 apple, cored and diced
½ teaspoon salt
2 cups fresh firm-textured
white bread crumbs
Curly endive
Plum slices

Cut pocket in each chop using tip of thin, sharp knife. Combine ¼ cup vermouth, 2 tablespoons fresh sage (or 2 teaspoons rubbed sage), soy sauce, oil, garlic and ¼ teaspoon pepper in glass dish; add pork chops, turning to coat. Heat butter in large skillet over medium heat until foamy. Add onion and apple; cook and stir about 6 minutes until onion is tender. Stir in remaining ½ cup vermouth, 2 tablespoons sage, ¼ teaspoon pepper and salt. Cook and stir over high heat about 3 minutes until liquid is almost gone. Transfer onion mixture to large bowl. Stir in bread crumbs.

Remove pork chops from marinade; discard marinade. Spoon onion mixture into pockets of pork chops. Close openings with wooden picks. (Soak wooden picks in hot water 15 minutes to prevent burning.) Grill pork chops on covered grill over medium Kingsford briquets about 5 minutes per side until barely pink in center. Garnish with endive and plum slices.

Makes 6 servings

Nutrients per Serving: Calories: 83, protein: 25 g, fat: 14 g, carbohydrate: 33 g, sodium: 614 mg, cholesterol: 71 mg

**Pork Chop with
Apple-Sage Stuffing**

Cajun Grilled Shrimp

Frozen shelled and deveined shrimp are a
great time-saver; just thaw and cook them.

3 green onions, minced
2 tablespoons lemon juice
3 cloves garlic, minced
2 teaspoons paprika
1 teaspoon salt
$\frac{1}{4}$ to $\frac{1}{2}$ teaspoon black pepper

$\frac{1}{4}$ to $\frac{1}{2}$ teaspoon cayenne
  pepper
1 tablespoon olive oil
$1\frac{1}{2}$ pounds shrimp, shelled with
  tails intact, deveined
Lemon wedges

Combine onions, lemon juice, garlic, paprika, salt and peppers in 2-quart
glass dish; stir in oil. Add shrimp; turn to coat. Cover and refrigerate at
least 15 minutes. Thread shrimp onto metal or wooden skewers. (Soak
wooden skewers in hot water 30 minutes to prevent burning.) Grill
shrimp over medium-hot Kingsford briquets about 2 minutes per side
until opaque. Serve immediately with lemon wedges.

Makes 4 servings

Nutrients per Serving: Calories: 139, protein: 26 g, fat: 3 g, carbohydrate: 1 g,
sodium: 189 mg, cholesterol: 194 mg

Cajun Grilled Shrimp

Grilled Flank Steak

Use leftover flank steak in salads, sandwiches and burritos.

½ cup soy sauce
3 tablespoons packed brown
  sugar
3 tablespoons lime juice
2 tablespoons dry sherry
  (optional)

1 tablespoon grated fresh
  ginger *or* 1 teaspoon
  ground ginger
3 cloves garlic, minced
1 beef flank steak
  (1½ to 2 pounds)

Stir together soy sauce, sugar, lime juice, sherry, ginger and garlic until sugar is dissolved. Reserve ¼ cup marinade for basting. Place beef in large resealable plastic food storage bag; add remaining marinade. Seal bag; turn to coat evenly. Marinate in refrigerator several hours or overnight. Remove beef from marinade; discard marinade. Grill beef on covered grill over medium-hot Kingsford briquets 12 to 14 minutes until medium-rare or to desired doneness, turning once and basting with reserved ¼ cup marinade. Slice steak diagonally across grain into thin slices.

Makes 6 to 8 servings

Nutrients per Serving (⅛ of recipe): Calories: 168, protein: 17 g, fat: 10 g, carbohydrate: 2 g, sodium: 345 mg, cholesterol: 46 mg

Grilled Turkey

**Sage-Garlic Baste (page 27)
  or Chinese 5-Spice Butter
  Baste (page 27)**

1 whole turkey (9 to 13
  pounds), thawed if frozen
  Salt and black pepper
3 lemons, halved (optional)

Prepare Sage-Garlic Baste. Remove neck and giblets from turkey. Rinse turkey under cold running water; pat dry with paper towels. Season turkey cavity with salt and pepper; place lemons in cavity, if desired. Lightly brush outer surface of turkey with part of Sage-Garlic Baste. Pull skin over neck and secure with skewer. Tuck wing tips under back and tie legs together with cotton string. Insert meat thermometer into thickest part of thigh, not touching bone. Arrange medium-hot Kingsford briquets on each side of large rectangular metal or foil drip pan. Pour hot tap water into drip pan until half full. Place turkey, breast side up, on grid directly above drip pan. Grill turkey on covered grill 9 to 13 minutes per pound or until thermometer registers 180°F, basting every 20 minutes with remaining Sage-Garlic Baste. Add a few briquets to both sides of fire every hour or as necessary to maintain constant temperature.* Let turkey stand 15 minutes before carving. Refrigerate leftovers promptly.

Makes 8 to 10 servings

For larger turkey, add 15 briquets every 50 to 60 minutes.

Sage-Garlic Baste

Grated peel and juice of
1 lemon
3 tablespoons olive oil
2 tablespoons minced fresh
sage *or* 1½ teaspoons
rubbed sage

2 cloves garlic, minced
½ teaspoon salt
¼ teaspoon black pepper

Combine all ingredients in small saucepan; cook and stir over medium heat 4 minutes. Use as baste for turkey or chicken.

Makes about ½ cup

Chinese 5-Spice Butter Baste

⅓ cup melted butter
1 tablespoon soy sauce

2 teaspoons Chinese 5-spice
powder

Combine all ingredients in small bowl. Use as baste for turkey or chicken.

Makes about 6 tablespoons

Nutrients per Serving (1/10 of Grilled Turkey with Sage-Garlic Baste): Calories: 194, protein: 34 g, fat: 5 g, carbohydrate: 0 g, sodium: 106 mg, cholesterol: 79 mg

Nutrients per Serving (1/10 of Grilled Turkey with Chinese 5-Spice Butter Baste): Calories: 204, protein: 34 g, fat: 7 g, carbohydrate: 0 g, sodium: 166 mg, cholesterol: 86 mg

Entertaining

Garlic-Pepper Skewered Pork

*This skewered pork recipe requires only half of a
2½-pound boneless pork loin roast. The remainder of the
roast is cut into chops, marinated, grilled and refrigerated;
use the chops another day to prepare Thai Pork Salad (page 42).*

1 boneless pork loin roast
    (about 2½ pounds)
6 to 15 cloves garlic, minced
⅓ cup lime juice
3 tablespoons firmly packed
    brown sugar

3 tablespoons soy sauce
2 tablespoons vegetable oil
2 teaspoons black pepper
¼ teaspoon cayenne pepper
8 green onions, cut into
    2-inch pieces (optional)

Cut pork crosswise into six ½-inch-thick chops, reserving remaining
roast. (Each chop may separate into 2 pieces.) Set chops aside in
13×9×2-inch glass dish. Cut remaining pork roast lengthwise into
2 pieces. Cut each piece into ⅛-inch-thick strips; place in dish with chops.
To prepare marinade, combine all remaining ingredients except green
onions in small bowl. Pour marinade over pork chops and slices; cover
and refrigerate at least 1 hour or overnight. Thread pork slices ribbon
style onto metal skewers, alternating pork with green onions. Grill
skewered pork slices and chops over medium-hot Kingsford briquets
about 3 minutes per side until no longer pink in center. (Chops may
require 1 to 2 minutes longer.) *Do not overcook.* Serve skewered pork
immediately. Cover and refrigerate chops for Thai Pork Salad (page 42).

*Makes 4 to 6 servings
(plus 6 chops for Thai Pork Salad)*

Nutrients per Serving: (⅙ of recipe): Calories: 247, protein: 23 g, fat: 13 g, carbohydrate: 7 g,
sodium: 425 mg, cholesterol: 73 mg

Grilled Paella

1½ to 2 pounds chicken wings
    or thighs
2 tablespoons plus ¼ cup
    extra-virgin olive oil,
    divided
  Salt and black pepper
1 pound garlicky sausage
    links, such as linguisa,
    chorizo or Italian
1 large onion, chopped
2 large red bell peppers,
    seeded and cut into thin
    strips
4 cloves garlic, minced

1 can (14 ounces) diced
    tomatoes, undrained
4 cups uncooked rice
16 tightly closed live mussels
    or clams,* scrubbed
½ pound large shrimp,* peeled
    and deveined with tails
    intact
1½ cups frozen peas
1 can (about 14 ounces)
    chicken broth
2 lemons, cut into wedges
1 oval disposable foil pan
    (about 17×13×3 inches)

Brush chicken with 2 tablespoons oil; season with salt and black pepper.
Grill chicken and sausage on covered grill over medium Kingsford
briquets 15 to 20 minutes or until chicken juices run clear and sausage is
no longer pink, turning every 5 minutes. Cut sausage into 2-inch pieces.

Heat remaining ¼ cup oil in large skillet over medium-high heat. Add
onion, bell peppers and garlic; cook and stir 5 minutes or until vegetables
are tender. Add tomatoes, 1½ teaspoons salt and ½ teaspoon black pepper;
cook about 8 minutes until thick, stirring frequently. Combine onion
mixture and rice in foil pan; spread evenly. Arrange chicken, sausage,
seafood and peas over rice. Bring broth and 6 cups water to a boil in
3 quart saucepan. Place foil pan on grid over medium Kingsford briquets;
immediately pour boiling broth mixture over rice. Grill on covered grill
about 20 minutes until liquid is absorbed. *Do not stir.* Cover with foil; let
stand 10 minutes. Garnish with lemon wedges.

Makes 8 to 10 servings

*Seafood can be omitted; add an additional 1¼ to 1½ pounds chicken.

Nutrients per Serving (¹⁄₁₀ of recipe): Calories: 572, protein: 26 g, fat: 22 g, carbohydrate: 67 g,
sodium: 875 mg, cholesterol: 82 mg

Grilled Paella

Jamaican Jerk Chicken

⅔ cup chopped green onions
3 tablespoons minced fresh
　　thyme leaves *or*
　　1 tablespoon dried thyme
　　leaves
3 tablespoons peanut oil
3 tablespoons soy sauce
2 tablespoons minced fresh
　　ginger
1 tablespoon minced garlic
1 habañero pepper, seeded and
　　minced *or* 1 tablespoon
　　minced, seeded serrano
　　pepper

1 bay leaf
1 teaspoon freshly ground
　　black pepper
1 teaspoon whole coriander
½ teaspoon ground nutmeg
½ teaspoon ground allspice
4 skinless boneless chicken
　　breast halves (4 to
　　6 ounces each)

To prepare marinade, combine all ingredients except chicken in small bowl; mix well. Place chicken in glass dish. Coat chicken with marinade. Marinate in refrigerator, several hours or overnight. Remove chicken from marinade; discard marinade. Grill chicken on covered grill over medium Kingsford briquets 4 to 6 minutes per side or until juices run clear.

Makes 4 servings

Nutrients per Serving: Calories: 226, protein: 23 g, fat: 13 g, carbohydrate: 5 g, sodium: 740 mg, cholesterol: 57 mg

Beef with Dry Spice Rub

3 tablespoons firmly packed
　　brown sugar
1 tablespoon black
　　peppercorns
1 tablespoon yellow mustard
　　seeds
1 tablespoon whole coriander
　　seeds

4 cloves garlic
1½ to 2 pounds beef top round
　　steak or London Broil,
　　about ½ inch thick
Vegetable or olive oil
Salt

Place sugar, peppercorns, mustard seeds, coriander seeds and garlic in blender or food processor; process until seeds and garlic are crushed. Rub beef with oil; pat on spice mixture. Season generously with salt.

Lightly oil hot grid to prevent sticking. Grill beef on covered grill over medium-low Kingsford briquets 16 to 20 minutes for medium or until desired doneness, turning once. Let stand 5 minutes before cutting across the grain into thin diagonal slices. *Makes 6 servings*

Nutrients per Serving: Calories: 249, protein: 29 g, fat: 11 g, carbohydrate: 9 g, sodium: 106 mg, cholesterol: 73 mg

Tuna Tacos with Grilled Pineapple Salsa

Grilled fish topped with fruit salsa has become standard fare at trendy restaurants. This recipe wraps tasty morsels of grilled tuna and a fiery pineapple salsa in corn tortillas for delicious soft tacos.

Tuna Vera Cruz (page 52)
½ **large pineapple, peeled, cored and cut into ½-inch thick slices**
8 **corn tortillas**
½ **medium red onion, cut into thin slivers**
¼ **cup cilantro leaves, chopped**

1 **tablespoon lime juice**
1 **to 3 teaspoons minced, seeded jalapeño pepper**
1 **garlic clove, minced**
¼ **teaspoon salt**
¼ **teaspoon freshly ground black pepper**

Prepare Tuna Vera Cruz; keep warm. Grill pineapple over medium-hot Kingsford briquets about 2 minutes per side until lightly browned. Grill tortillas until hot but not crisp; keep warm. Cut grilled pineapple into ½-inch cubes. Combine pineapple, onion, cilantro, lime juice, jalapeño pepper, garlic, salt and black pepper in medium bowl. Break tuna into bite-size chunks. Spoon pineapple salsa down center of each tortilla; top with tuna. Roll to enclose. Serve immediately. *Makes 4 servings*

Nutrients per Serving (2 tacos): Calories: 438, protein: 44 g, fat: 10 g, carbohydrate: 44, sodium: 296 mg, cholesterol: 64 mg

Herbed Butter Chicken

A mixture of fresh herbs, garlic and lemon peel tucked under the skin before grilling adds a flavor punch to chicken.

3 tablespoons minced fresh
    basil
2 teaspoons minced fresh
    oregano
2 teaspoons minced fresh
    rosemary
3 tablespoons minced shallots
    or green onion
2 tablespoons butter, softened
3 cloves garlic, minced

2 teaspoons grated lemon peel
½ teaspoon salt
¼ teaspoon black pepper
4 chicken legs with thighs *or*
    1 whole chicken (about
    3½ pounds), quartered
1 tablespoon olive oil
    Fresh oregano sprigs
    Lemon peel strips

Combine herbs, shallots, butter, garlic, lemon peel, salt and pepper in medium bowl. Loosen chicken skin by gently pushing fingers between the skin and chicken, keeping skin intact. Gently rub herb mixture under skin of chicken, forcing it into the leg section; secure skin with wooden picks. (Soak wooden picks in hot water 15 minutes to prevent burning.) Cover and refrigerate chicken at least ½ hour. Brush chicken with oil. Arrange medium Kingsford briquets on each side of rectangular metal or foil drip pan. Grill chicken, skin side down, in center of grid on covered grill 20 minutes. Turn chicken and cook 20 to 25 minutes or until juices run clear. Garnish with oregano sprigs and lemon strips.   *Makes 4 servings*

Nutrients per Serving: Calories: 347, protein: 30 g, fat: 24 g, carbohydrate: 2 g, sodium: 450 mg, cholesterol: 119 mg

Herbed Butter Chicken

Pork Tenderloin with Grilled Apple Cream Sauce

This delicate, lean pork tenderloin should be cooked just until it is barely pink in the center. Overcooking will cause pork to become dry.

1 can (6 ounces) frozen apple juice concentrate, thawed and divided (¾ cup)
½ cup Calvados or brandy, divided
2 tablespoons Dijon mustard
1 tablespoon olive oil
3 cloves garlic, minced
1¼ teaspoons salt, divided

¼ teaspoon black pepper
1½ pounds pork tenderloin
2 green or red apples, cored
1 tablespoon butter
½ large red onion, cut into thin slivers
½ cup heavy cream
Fresh thyme sprigs

Reserve 2 tablespoons juice concentrate. Combine remaining juice concentrate, ¼ cup Calvados, mustard, oil, garlic, 1 teaspoon salt and pepper in glass dish. Add pork; turn to coat. Cover and refrigerate 2 hours, turning pork occasionally. Cut apples crosswise into ⅜-inch rings. Remove pork from marinade; discard marinade. Grill pork on covered grill over medium Kingsford briquets about 20 minutes, turning 3 times, until meat thermometer inserted in thickest part registers 155°F. Grill apples about 4 minutes per side until tender; cut rings into quarters. Melt butter in large skillet over medium heat. Add onion; cook and stir until soft. Stir in apples, remaining ¼ cup Calvados, ¼ teaspoon salt and reserved 2 tablespoons apple juice. Add cream; heat through. Cut pork crosswise into ½-inch slices; spoon sauce over pork. Garnish with fresh thyme.

Makes 4 servings

Nutrients per Serving: Calories: 462, protein: 40 g, fat: 21 g, carbohydrate: 19 g, sodium: 279 mg, cholesterol: 174 mg

Pork Tenderloin with Grilled Apple Cream Sauce

Beef Direct Grilling Chart

Beef Cut (cooked yield per pound)	Thickness/ Weight	Approximate Cooking Time (uncovered over medium coals; medium-rare to medium doneness)
Tenderloin Steak Yields 4 (3-ounce) servings of cooked, trimmed beef per pound.	1 inch 1½ inches	13 to 15 minutes 14 to 16 minutes (covered)
Top Round Steak Yields 4 (3-ounce) servings of cooked, trimmed beef per pound.	¾ inch 1 inch 1½ inches	8 to 9 minutes* 16 to 18 minutes* 25 to 28 minutes* (covered)
Ground Beef Patties Yields 4 (3-ounce) servings of cooked beef per pound.**	½ × 4 inches	14 to 16 minutes
Boneless Top Loin Steak Yields 3¾ (3-ounce) servings of cooked, trimmed beef per pound.	¾ inch 1 inch	10 to 12 minutes 15 to 18 minutes
Boneless Top Sirloin Steak Yields 3½ (3-ounce) servings of cooked, trimmed beef per pound.	¾ inch 1 inch 1½ inches 2 inches	13 to 16 minutes 17 to 21 minutes 22 to 26 minutes (covered) 28 to 33 minutes (covered)
Chuck Shoulder Steak Yields 3½ (3-ounce) servings of cooked, trimmed beef per pound.	¾ inch 1 inch	14 to 17 minutes 16 to 20 minutes
Chuck Top Blade Steak Yields 3 (3-ounce) servings of cooked, trimmed beef per pound.	1 inch	18 to 22 minutes
Flank Steak Yields 4 (3-ounce) servings of cooked, trimmed beef per pound.	1½ to 2 pounds	17 to 21 minutes
Porterhouse/T-Bone Steak Yields 2½ (3-ounce) servings of cooked, trimmed beef per pound.	¾ inch 1 inch	10 to 12 minutes 14 to 16 minutes
Ribeye Steak Yields 3 (3-ounce) servings of cooked, trimmed beef per pound.	¾ inch 1 inch 1½ inches	6 to 8 minutes 11 to 14 minutes 17 to 22 minutes (covered)

Note: All cook times are based on beef removed directly from the refrigerator.

*Cook top round steak to medium-rare (145°F) doneness only.
**USDA recommends cooking ground beef patties to medium (160°F) doneness.

Chart courtesy of National Cattlemen's Beef Association.

Grilled Caribbean Steaks

Rubbing a dry marinade on meat results in a more intense flavor than a liquid marinade. For best flavor in this recipe, rub the steaks with the herb and spice mixture two or three days before cooking.

6 tablespoons brown sugar
2½ tablespoons paprika
2 tablespoons granulated
    sugar
1 tablespoon kosher salt
1 tablespoon chili powder
1¼ teaspoons granulated garlic
    or garlic powder
1¼ teaspoons dried oregano
    leaves

1¼ teaspoons dried basil leaves
¾ teaspoon dried thyme leaves
¾ teaspoon celery seed
¼ teaspoon cayenne pepper
2 lean beef T-bone steaks
    (12 to 16 ounces each),
    1 inch thick

To prepare spice mix, combine all ingredients except steak in small bowl; mix well. Measure out ¼ cup spice mix, reserving remaining for other uses.* Rub steaks with ¼ cup spice mix, using 1 tablespoon per side. Refrigerate steaks, covered, overnight or up to 3 days. Grill steaks on covered grill over medium Kingsford briquets 12 to 14 minutes for medium-rare or to desired doneness, turning once.

Makes 4 to 6 servings

*Recipe for spice mix makes 1¼ cups. Store leftover spice mix in covered container in cool, dry place. Use with beef, pork or chicken.

Nutrients per Serving (⅙ of recipe): Calories: 205, protein: 25 g, fat: 9 g, carbohydrate: 3 g, sodium: 297 mg, cholesterol: 72 mg

Grilled Fish with Orange-Chile Salsa

3 medium oranges, peeled and
  sectioned* (about
  1¼ cups segments)
¼ cup finely diced green, red
  or yellow bell pepper
3 tablespoons chopped
  cilantro, divided
3 tablespoons lime juice,
  divided
1 tablespoon honey

1 teaspoon minced, seeded
  serrano pepper *or*
1 tablespoon minced
  jalapeño pepper
1¼ pounds firm white fish
  fillets, such as orange
  roughy, lingcod, halibut
  or red snapper
Lime slices
Zucchini ribbons, cooked

To prepare Orange-Chile Salsa, combine orange segments, bell pepper,
2 tablespoons cilantro, 2 tablespoons lime juice, honey and serrano
pepper. Set aside.

Season fish fillets with remaining 1 tablespoon cilantro and 1 tablespoon
lime juice. Lightly oil grid to prevent sticking. Grill fish on covered grill
over medium Kingsford briquets 5 minutes. Turn and top with lime slices,
if desired. Grill about 5 minutes until fish flakes easily when tested with
fork. Serve with Orange-Chile Salsa. Garnish with zucchini ribbons.

Makes 4 servings

*Canned mandarin orange segments can be substituted for fresh orange segments, if desired.

Note: Allow about 10 minutes grilling time per inch thickness of fish
fillets.

Nutrients per Serving: Calories: 206, protein: 30 g, fat: 3 g, carbohydrate: 13 g,
sodium: 79 mg, cholesterol: 46 mg

Grilled Fish with Orange-Chile Salsa

Thai Pork Salad

This salad is perfect for a quick dinner if the pork chops
are grilled when preparing Garlic-Pepper Skewered Pork (page 28);
otherwise grill boneless pork chops.

8 cups lightly packed
   shredded cabbage or
   packaged coleslaw mix
1 cup lightly packed cilantro
   leaves, coarsely chopped
30 large mint leaves, coarsely
   chopped
6 grilled pork loin chops
   (from Garlic-Pepper
   Skewered Pork, page 28)
   or 6 grilled ½-inch-thick
   boneless pork chops
2 tablespoons vegetable oil

½ large red onion, cut into
   thin slivers
½ cup lightly salted roasted
   cashews or peanuts
½ teaspoon salt
¼ to ½ teaspoon cayenne
   pepper
⅓ cup lime juice
1 tablespoon sugar
   Lime wedges
   Red onion strips
   Cilantro sprigs

Combine cabbage, cilantro and mint in large bowl; set aside. Cut pork
chops into ¼-inch-thick strips. Heat oil in large skillet over medium-high
heat. Add pork, onion, nuts, salt and cayenne pepper. Cook and stir
2 minutes; remove from heat. Stir in lime juice and sugar. Spoon pork
mixture over cabbage; toss well to coat. Garnish with lime wedges, onion
strips and cilantro.

Makes 5 main-dish servings
or 8 to 10 side-dish servings

Nutrients per Serving (1 main-dish serving): Calories: 281, protein: 18 g, fat: 15 g,
carbohydrate: 21 g, sodium: 496 mg, cholesterol: 41 mg

Thai Pork Salad

Express

Rosemary Steak

The aromatic combination of rosemary, garlic and lemon peel evokes the sun-drenched cuisines of the Mediterranean region. For a special meal, serve Rosemary Steak with grilled potato slices or garlic mashed potatoes and drizzle with Balsamic-Mushroom Vinaigrette (page 51).

4 boneless top loin beef steaks or New York strip steaks (about 6 ounces each)
2 tablespoons minced fresh rosemary
2 cloves garlic, minced
1 tablespoon extra-virgin olive oil

1 teaspoon grated lemon peel
1 teaspoon coarsely ground black pepper
½ teaspoon salt
Fresh rosemary sprigs

Score steaks in diamond pattern on both sides. Combine minced rosemary, garlic, oil, lemon peel, pepper and salt in small bowl; rub mixture onto surface of meat. Cover and refrigerate at least 15 minutes. Grill steaks over medium-hot Kingsford briquets about 4 minutes per side until medium-rare or to desired doneness. Cut steaks diagonally into ½-inch-thick slices. Garnish with rosemary sprigs. *Makes 4 servings*

Nutrients per Serving: Calories: 328, protein: 42 g, fat: 16 g, carbohydrate: 1 g, sodium: 392 mg, cholesterol: 110 mg

Rosemary Steak

Turkey Teriyaki Udon

Udon and soba are Japanese-style noodles. Udon is made
from wheat and soba from buckwheat. They are available fresh and
dried in Asian markets and dried in some large supermarkets.
Linguine can be substituted.

Turkey Teriyaki with Grilled
   Mushrooms (page 56)
12 ounces fresh udon or soba
   noodles
3 cups water
1 can (14 ounces) chicken
   broth
2 tablespoons sake or sherry
   wine

1 tablespoon minced fresh
   ginger
1 tablespoon soy sauce
2 teaspoons sugar
1½ cups chopped fresh or
   frozen spinach, thawed
1 cup fresh bean sprouts
   Carrot flowers

Prepare Turkey Teriyaki with Grilled Mushrooms. Cook noodles according
to package directions; drain and keep warm. Combine water, broth, sake,
ginger, soy sauce and sugar in 5-quart Dutch oven. Bring to a boil over
high heat. Reduce heat to medium-low and simmer 5 minutes. Stir in
spinach and bean sprouts; heat through. Place noodles in 4 large soup
bowls; spoon broth mixture over noodles. Slice turkey into bite-size
pieces; arrange turkey, mushrooms and green onions on noodles. Garnish
with carrot flowers. Serve immediately.   *Makes 4 servings*

Nutrients per Serving: Calories: 398, protein: 44 g, fat: 4 g, carbohydrate: 46 g,
sodium: 830 mg, cholesterol: 89 mg

Turkey Teriyaki Udon

Southwest Chicken

Prepare a double recipe–the leftovers make great beginnings for quick weekday meals.

2 tablespoons olive oil
1 clove garlic, pressed
1 teaspoon chili powder
1 teaspoon ground cumin
1 teaspoon dried oregano
   leaves

½ teaspoon salt
1 pound skinless boneless
   chicken breast halves or
   thighs

Combine oil, garlic, chili powder, cumin, oregano and salt; brush over both sides of chicken to coat. Grill chicken over medium-hot Kingsford briquets 8 to 10 minutes or until chicken is no longer pink, turning once. Serve immediately or use in Build a Burrito, Taco Salad or other favorite recipes.

Makes 4 servings

Note: Southwest Chicken can be grilled ahead and refrigerated for several days or frozen for longer storage.

Build a Burrito: Top warm large flour tortillas with strips of Southwest Chicken and your choice of drained canned black beans, cooked brown or white rice, shredded cheese, salsa verde, shredded lettuce, sliced black olives and chopped cilantro. Fold in sides and roll to enclose filling. Heat in microwave oven at HIGH until heated through. (Or, wrap in foil and heat in preheated 350°F oven.)

Taco Salad: For a quick one-dish meal, layer strips of Southwest Chicken with tomato wedges, blue or traditional corn tortilla chips, sliced black olives, shredded romaine or iceberg lettuce, shredded cheese and avocado slices. Serve with salsa, sour cream, guacamole or a favorite dressing.

Nutrients per Serving (Southwest Chicken): Calories: 202, protein: 26 g, fat: 10 g, carbohydrate: 1 g, sodium: 362 mg, cholesterol: 70 mg

Taco Salad

Peanut Pork Lo Mein

Lo mein, a popular Chinese dish, consists of
boiled noodles, pork or chicken and vegetables seasoned
with a flavorful sauce. This sensational version has the added
dimension of smoky grilled pork and vegetables.

½ recipe Peanut Pork
Tenderloin (page 59), hot
and sliced into bite-size
pieces *or* ¾ pound pork
tenderloin, grilled and
sliced into bite-size pieces

1 package (12 ounces) fresh
chow mein noodles or
linguine

1 red bell pepper, cut into thin
slivers

1 small red onion, cut into
thin slivers

1½ cups snow peas, cut in half
diagonally

2 cloves garlic, minced

8 teaspoons vegetable oil,
divided

Salt and freshly ground
black pepper

2 tablespoons rice vinegar

2 tablespoons oyster sauce

2 tablespoons soy sauce

1 tablespoon dark sesame oil

2 green onions, thinly sliced
on diagonal

Prepare Peanut Pork Tenderloin. Cook noodles according to package
directions; drain and place in large bowl. Meanwhile, place bell pepper,
onion, snow peas and garlic in center of 18×12-inch sheet of heavy-duty
foil; drizzle with 2 teaspoons vegetable oil and season to taste with salt
and black pepper. Bring edges of foil up to form shallow pan. Grill
vegetables in foil pan on covered grill over medium Kingsford briquets
about 10 minutes until vegetables are crisp-tender, stirring gently several
times. Whisk together vinegar, oyster sauce, soy sauce, sesame oil and
remaining 6 teaspoons vegetable oil; pour over noodles, tossing to coat.
Arrange noodle mixture on large platter. Top with pork and vegetables;
garnish with green onions. Serve immediately.   *Makes 4 servings*

Nutrients per Serving: Calories: 466, protein: 29 g, fat: 18 g, carbohydrate: 47 g,
sodium: 1002 mg, cholesterol: 62 mg

Minty Lemon Chicken Soup

2 grilled Lemon-Garlic
   Chicken breast halves
   (page 54) or 2 grilled
   chicken breast halves
6 cups chicken broth, divided

1 cup uncooked long-grain rice
¼ cup lemon juice
¼ cup chopped fresh mint
Salt and black pepper

Prepare Lemon-Garlic Chicken. Bring 2 cups of chicken broth to a boil in large saucepan. Add rice; reduce heat to low and cook, covered, 15 minutes or until liquid has been absorbed. Stir in remaining 4 cups broth and lemon juice. Bring to a boil over high heat. Cut chicken into thin strips. Stir in chicken and mint. Season to taste with salt and pepper.

Makes 4 servings (about 2 cups each)

Nutrients per Serving: Calories: 331, protein: 24 g, fat: 7 g, carbohydrate: 40 g, sodium: 1344 mg, cholesterol: 35 mg

Balsamic-Mushroom Vinaigrette

Simmering mushrooms in balsamic vinegar
gives this vinaigrette a rich mushroom flavor,
which complements grilled beef, fish and poultry.

5 tablespoons extra-virgin
   olive oil, divided
¼ pound mushrooms, finely
   chopped
¼ cup water

2 tablespoons balsamic
   vinegar
1 teaspoon Dijon mustard
¼ teaspoon salt
3 tablespoons lemon juice

Heat 1 tablespoon oil in medium skillet over medium-high heat. Add mushrooms; cook and stir about 7 minutes until brown. Combine water, vinegar, mustard and salt in small bowl; add to mushrooms in skillet. Simmer until liquid is reduced by half. Remove from heat; whisk in lemon juice and remaining 4 tablespoons oil. Drizzle over grilled meats, poultry or fish.

Makes ¾ cup

Nutrients per Serving (3 tablespoons): Calories: 108, protein: trace, fat: 11 g, carbohydrate: 2 g, sodium: 123 mg, cholesterol: 0 mg

Tuna Vera Cruz

For a head start on tomorrow's dinner, prepare
a double recipe of this zesty tuna dish. Serve half
tonight and refrigerate the remaining tuna to make
Tuna Tacos with Grilled Pineapple Salsa (page 33).

3 tablespoons tequila, rum or
   vodka
2 tablespoons lime juice
2 teaspoons grated lime peel
1 piece (1-inch cube) fresh
   ginger, minced
2 cloves garlic, minced
1 teaspoon salt
1 teaspoon sugar

½ teaspoon ground cumin
¼ teaspoon ground cinnamon
¼ teaspoon black pepper
1 tablespoon vegetable oil
1½ pounds fresh tuna, halibut,
   swordfish or shark steaks
Lemon and lime wedges
Fresh rosemary sprigs

Combine tequila, lime juice, lime peel, ginger, garlic, salt, sugar, cumin,
cinnamon and pepper in 2-quart glass dish; stir in oil. Add tuna; turn
to coat. Cover and refrigerate at least 30 minutes. Remove tuna from
marinade; discard marinade. Grill tuna over medium-hot Kingsford
briquets about 4 minutes per side until fish flakes easily when tested
with fork. Garnish with lemon wedges, lime wedges and rosemary sprigs.

Makes 4 servings

Nutrients per Serving: Calories: 249, protein: 40 g, fat: 9 g, carbohydrate: 0 g,
sodium: 66 mg, cholesterol: 65 mg

Tuna Vera Cruz

Lemon-Garlic Chicken

*Grill an extra pound of chicken breast halves to use
for another meal of Minty Lemon Chicken Soup (page 51)
or Pasta Express (page 58) later in the week.*

2 tablespoons olive oil
2 cloves garlic, pressed
1 teaspoon grated lemon peel
1 teaspoon lemon juice
¼ teaspoon salt

¼ teaspoon black pepper
4 skinless boneless chicken
   breast halves (about
   1 pound)

Combine oil, garlic, lemon peel, lemon juice, salt and pepper in small
bowl. Brush oil mixture over both sides of chicken to coat. Lightly oil grid
to prevent sticking. Grill chicken over medium Kingsford briquets 8 to
10 minutes or until chicken is no longer pink in center, turning once.

Makes 4 servings

Nutrients per Serving: Calories: 199, protein: 26 g, fat: 10 g, carbohydrate: 1 g,
sodium: 208 mg, cholesterol: 70 mg

 ## Sure-Fire Dessert

Barbecue Banana Split: Cut firm, ripe banana
lengthwise to, but not through, bottom peel. Brush cut sides with
melted butter; sprinkle with a little brown sugar. Grill 6 to
8 minutes on covered grill over medium-hot Kingsford briquets until
banana is heated through but still firm (peel will turn dark). Place
unpeeled banana in serving dish; top with small scoops of ice cream.
Drizzle with chocolate or caramel sauce. Top with whipped cream,
nuts and a cherry.

Backyard S'Mores

2 milk chocolate bars
  (1.55 ounces each),
  cut in half

8 large marshmallows
4 whole graham crackers
  (8 squares)

Place each chocolate bar half and 2 marshmallows between 2 graham cracker squares. Wrap in lightly greased foil. Place on grill over medium-low Kingsford briquets about 3 to 5 minutes or until chocolate and marshmallows are melted. (Time will vary depending upon how hot coals are and whether grill is open or covered.)   *Makes 4 servings*

Nutrients per Serving: Calories: 224, protein: 3 g, fat: 8 g, carbohydrate: 37 g, sodium: 117 mg, cholesterol: 6 mg

Grilled Fish with
Roasted Jalapeño Rub

(Recipe adapted from Chef Randall Warder,
Mansion on Turtle Creek, Dallas, TX)

3 tablespoons chopped
  cilantro
2 tablespoons lime juice
1 tablespoon minced garlic
1 tablespoon minced fresh
  ginger

1 tablespoon minced roasted
  jalapeño peppers*
1½ pounds firm white fish
  fillets, such as orange
  roughy or red snapper
Lime wedges

Combine cilantro, lime juice, garlic, ginger and pepper in small bowl. Lightly oil grid to prevent sticking. Grill fish on covered grill over hot Kingsford briquets 5 minutes. Turn; spread cilantro mixture on fish. Grill 3 to 5 minutes longer or until fish flakes easily when tested with fork. Serve with lime wedges.   *Makes 4 servings*

*To roast peppers, place them on uncovered grill over hot coals. Grill until blistered, turning frequently. Remove from grill and place in large resealable plastic food storage bag for 15 minutes. Remove skins. Seed peppers, if desired, and cut into thin slices.

Nutrients per Serving: Calories: 236, protein: 33 g, fat: 10 g, carbohydrate: 2 g, sodium: 88 mg, cholesterol: 102 mg

Turkey Teriyaki with Grilled Mushrooms

Serve this dish right from the grill or use it to prepare Turkey Teriyaki Udon (page 46).

1¼ pounds turkey breast slices,
  tenderloins or medallions
¼ cup sake or sherry wine
¼ cup soy sauce
3 tablespoons granulated
  sugar, brown sugar or
  honey

1 piece (1-inch cube) fresh
  ginger, minced
3 cloves garlic, minced
1 tablespoon vegetable oil
½ pound mushrooms
4 green onions, cut into
  2-inch pieces

Cut turkey into long 2-inch-wide strips.* Combine sake, soy sauce, sugar, ginger, garlic and oil in 2-quart glass dish. Add turkey; turn to coat. Cover and refrigerate 15 minutes or overnight. Remove turkey from marinade; discard marinade. Thread turkey onto metal or wooden skewers, alternating with mushrooms and green onions. (Soak wooden skewers in hot water 30 minutes to prevent burning.) Grill on covered grill over medium-hot Kingsford briquets about 3 minutes per side until turkey is cooked through.   *Makes 4 servings*

*Do not cut tenderloins or medallions.

Nutrients per Serving: Calories: 173, protein: 34 g, fat: 2 g, carbohydrate: 5 g, sodium: 160 mg, cholesterol: 89 mg

Turkey Teriyaki with
Grilled Mushrooms

Pasta Express

Serve with a deli salad and hot crusty bread for a quick dinner.

2 grilled Lemon-Garlic
    Chicken breast halves
    (page 54) or 2 plain
    grilled chicken breast
    halves
1 package (9 ounces) lemon-
    pepper or plain linguine
¼ cup olive oil
½ medium yellow onion, sliced

3 cloves garlic, minced
1 cup grilled red or yellow bell
    pepper strips
¼ cup chopped fresh basil
    or parsley
1 cup freshly grated Parmesan
    cheese
Salt and black pepper

Prepare Lemon-Garlic Chicken; cut into thin slices. Cook linguine according to package directions until al dente; drain. Place in large bowl; keep warm. Heat oil in large skillet over medium heat. Add onion and garlic; cook and stir onion until crisp-tender. Add chicken, onion mixture, bell pepper, basil and cheese to linguine; season to taste with salt and black pepper. Toss until well mixed. *Makes 3 to 4 servings*

Nutrients per Serving (¼ of recipe): Calories: 564, protein: 30 g, fat: 26 g, carbohydrate: 53 g, sodium: 556 mg, cholesterol: 51 mg

Sure-Fire Dessert

Grilled Pineapple: Peel, core and cut pineapple into ³⁄₄-inch-thick rings or thin wedges. Brush generously with dark rum; sprinkle with brown sugar. Lightly oil grid to prevent sticking. Grill 8 to 10 minutes over medium-hot Kingsford briquets until warm and golden brown, turning once. Top each ring with 1 scoop of ice cream, frozen yogurt or sorbet and a sprinkling of toasted coconut.

Peanut Pork Tenderloin

This Asian-inspired dish has flavors reminiscent
of Thai peanut sauce. Serve it with steamed rice and
grilled asparagus for a quick and easy meal.

⅓ cup chunky unsweetened
   peanut butter
⅓ cup regular or light canned
   coconut milk
¼ cup lemon juice or dry white
   wine
3 tablespoons soy sauce
3 cloves garlic, minced

2 tablespoons sugar
1 piece (1-inch cube) fresh
   ginger, minced
½ teaspoon salt
¼ to ½ teaspoon cayenne
   pepper
¼ teaspoon ground cinnamon
1½ pounds pork tenderloin

Combine peanut butter, coconut milk, lemon juice, soy sauce, garlic, sugar,
ginger, salt, cayenne pepper and cinnamon in 2-quart glass dish until
blended. Add pork; turn to coat. Cover and refrigerate at least 30 minutes
or overnight. Remove pork from marinade; discard marinade. Grill pork
on covered grill over medium Kingsford briquets about 20 minutes until
just barely pink in center, turning 4 times. Cut crosswise into ½-inch
slices. Serve immediately.   *Makes 4 to 6 servings*

Nutrients per Serving (⅙ of recipe): Calories: 248, protein: 39 g, fat: 8 g, carbohydrate: 2 g,
sodium: 217 mg, cholesterol: 125 mg

Vegetables, Salads & More

Sausage & Wilted Spinach Salad

¼ cup sherry vinegar or white wine vinegar

1 teaspoon whole mustard seeds, crushed

½ teaspoon salt

¼ teaspoon black pepper

2 ears corn, husked

1 large red onion, cut into ¾-inch-thick slices

4 tablespoons extra-virgin olive oil, divided

12 ounces smoked turkey, chicken or pork sausage links, such as Polish, Andouille or New Mexico style, cut in half lengthwise

2 cloves garlic, minced

10 cups lightly packed spinach leaves, torn

1 large avocado, peeled and cubed

Combine vinegar, mustard seeds, salt and pepper; set dressing aside. Brush corn and onion with 1 tablespoon oil. Insert wooden picks into onion slices from edges to prevent separating into rings. (Soak wooden picks in hot water 15 minutes to prevent burning.) Grill sausage, corn and onion over medium Kingsford briquets 6 to 10 minutes until vegetables are crisp-tender and sausage is hot, turning several times. Cut corn kernels from cobs; chop onion and slice sausage. Heat remaining 3 tablespoons oil in small skillet over medium heat. Add garlic; cook and stir 1 minute. Toss spinach, avocado, sausage, corn, onion and dressing in large bowl. Drizzle hot oil over salad; toss and serve immediately. *Makes 4 servings*

Nutrients per Serving: Calories: 477, protein: 16 g, fat: 37 g, carbohydrate: 26 g, sodium: 939 mg, cholesterol: 33 mg

Grilled Vegetable & Orzo Salad with Citrus Vinaigrette

½ cup thinly sliced shallots or green onions

⅓ cup white wine vinegar

¼ cup orange juice

2 tablespoons lemon juice

2 tablespoons extra-virgin olive oil

1½ teaspoons grated orange peel

1½ teaspoons grated lemon peel

1½ teaspoons salt

¼ teaspoon black pepper

10 large mushrooms, cut in half

1 package (10 ounces) frozen artichoke hearts, thawed

12 ounces orzo pasta, cooked, rinsed and drained

2 red or green bell peppers, cut in half, stemmed and seeded

12 large fresh basil leaves, minced (optional)

Orange peel strips

Combine shallots, vinegar, juices, oil, peels, salt and black pepper in large bowl; whisk until blended. Add mushrooms and artichokes; let stand 30 minutes. Thread artichokes and mushrooms onto wooden skewers; reserve vinaigrette. (Soak wooden skewers in hot water 30 minutes to prevent burning.) Add orzo to reserved dressing; toss to coat. Grill artichokes and mushrooms on covered grill over medium-hot Kingsford briquets 3 to 5 minutes per side. Grill bell peppers, skin sides down, over medium-hot briquets about 8 minutes until skins on all sides are charred. Place peppers in large resealable plastic food storage bag or paper bag; seal. Let stand 5 minutes; remove skin. Slice mushrooms and chop peppers; add to pasta with artichokes and basil, tossing until coated. Serve at room temperature. Garnish with orange peel strips.

Makes 8 side-dish servings (about 1 cup each)

Note: To make an entrée that serves four, add 1 can (15 ounces) rinsed and drained black beans *or* 2 cups cubed grilled chicken or sliced grilled sausage.

Nutrients per Serving: Calories: 209, protein: 7 g, fat: 13 g, carbohydrate: 16 g, sodium: 234 mg, cholesterol: 18 mg

Grilled Vegetable & Orzo Salad with Citrus Vinaigrette

Grilled Fresh Fruit

Fruit becomes slightly caramelized and picks up a
pleasant smoky flavor when cooked over smoldering coals.
Grilled fruit is a wonderful accompaniment to fish, poultry
and meat or a delicious topping for ice cream.

Fruit	Preparation for Grilling
Apples	cored and cut into ⅜-inch-thick rings
Apricots	cut in half and pitted
Cherries	pitted, if desired
Figs	whole or cut in half
Peaches and nectarines	peeled, if desired, pitted and sliced
Pears	cored and cut into ⅜-inch-thick rings
Pineapple	peeled, cored and cut into wedges or ½-inch-thick rings
Strawberries	large whole

Preparation: Brush fruit with melted butter or oil. Grill over medium-hot
Kingsford briquets 1 to 2 minutes per side or until lightly browned and
almost tender.

For a side dish: Place 2 cups grilled fruit slices or chunks in medium
bowl. Sprinkle with 2 tablespoons rice vinegar, 1 tablespoon olive oil and
2 teaspoons sugar; toss gently. *Makes 4 servings.*

For a dessert: Place 2 cups bite-size grilled fruit in a large bowl. Drizzle
with 1 to 2 tablespoons melted butter; toss gently. Sprinkle with
2 tablespoons sugar and drizzle with 4 tablespoons orange-flavored
liqueur. Serve over plain low-fat yogurt, vanilla ice cream or crème fraîche.
Makes 4 servings.

Grilled Banana Squash with Rum & Brown Sugar

Micro-grilling cuts grilling time in half. Partially cook the squash in a microwave oven and then finish cooking it on the grill.

2 pounds banana squash or
butternut squash
2 tablespoons dark rum or
apple juice

2 tablespoons melted butter
2 tablespoons brown sugar

Cut squash into 4 pieces; discard seeds. Place squash in microwavable baking dish. Cover with vented plastic wrap. Microwave at HIGH 5 to 7 minutes, turning once. Discard plastic wrap; pierce flesh of squash with fork at 1-inch intervals. Place squash in foil pan. Combine rum and butter; brush over squash. Sprinkle with sugar. Grill squash on covered grill over medium Kingsford briquets 20 to 30 minutes until squash is tender.

Makes 4 servings

Nutrients per Serving: Calories: 170, protein: 2 g, fat: 6 g, carbohydrate: 31 g, sodium: 69 mg, cholesterol: 16 mg

Mediterranean Grilled Vegetables

4 medium red or Yukon gold potatoes, cooked
3 tablespoons orange juice
2 tablespoons balsamic vinegar
1 clove garlic, minced
½ teaspoon salt
¼ teaspoon black pepper
⅓ cup plus 3 tablespoons olive oil, divided
8 thin slices (4×2 inches) prosciutto or ham (optional)
3 ounces soft goat cheese, cut into 8 pieces (optional)

8 asparagus spears
2 red or yellow bell peppers, cut in half, stemmed and seeded
2 zucchini, cut lengthwise into ¼-inch slices
2 Japanese eggplants, cut lengthwise into ¼-inch slices
1 fennel bulb, cut in half
8 large mushrooms
2 poblano or green bell peppers, cut in half, stemmed and seeded

Cut potatoes into thick slices. Combine juice, vinegar, garlic, salt and black pepper in small bowl; whisk in ⅓ cup oil. Set aside. Wrap each slice prosciutto around 1 piece cheese and 1 asparagus spear. Thread cheese bundles onto wooden skewers, piercing asparagus and securing cheese with wooden picks, if necessary. (Soak wooden skewers and picks in hot water 30 minutes to prevent burning.) Brush bundles with 3 tablespoons remaining oil.

Grill bell peppers, skin sides down, over medium Kingsford briquets 8 minutes until skins are charred. Place in large resealable plastic food storage bag; seal. Let stand 5 minutes; remove skin. Grill remaining vegetables on covered grill over medium briquets 2 to 5 minutes per side until tender. Grill cheese bundles over medium briquets until lightly browned. Arrange vegetables and cheese bundles in 13×9-inch glass dish; drizzle with dressing, turning to coat. Let stand 15 minutes.

Makes 6 to 8 servings

Nutrients per Serving (⅛ of recipe): Calories: 168, protein: 5 g, fat: 7 g, carbohydrate: 26 g, sodium: 27 mg, cholesterol: 0 mg

Mediterranean Grilled Vegetables

Grilled Vegetables

Vegetable	Preparation for Grilling	Grilling Time
Beans, green	whole	5 minutes
Bell peppers or chili peppers	whole or cut in half, stemmed and seeded	10 to 20 minutes
Corn on cob	remove silk; soak unhusked corn in cold water 30 minutes	20 to 30 minutes
Eggplant, Japanese, Chinese and Italian	cut lengthwise into halves	20 minutes
Eggplant, traditional Western	cut into 1-inch-thick rounds	20 minutes
Leeks	whole, trim ends and discard tough outer layers	15 to 20 minutes
Mushrooms	stems removed	10 minutes
Onions, dry (yellow, white or red)	peel and cut into halves, wedges or rounds (To prevent separating, insert wooden picks into onions.*)	20 to 30 minutes
Onions, green	whole; roots and tops trimmed off	5 minutes
Potatoes	cut into ½-inch-thick rounds	10 to 12 minutes
Squash, summer	cut into halves or thick slices	5 to 10 minutes
Tomatoes	cut into halves or thick slices	5 to 10 minutes

Preparation: Brush vegetables lightly with vegetable oil. Season with chopped fresh or dried herbs, if desired. Thread small vegetables and pieces onto metal or wooden skewers* or place in grill basket; place large vegetables on grid. Grill vegetables over medium Kingsford briquets or around edges of hot briquets until tender, turning occasionally.

*Soak wooden picks in hot water 15 minutes and wooden skewers 30 minutes to prevent burning.

Risotto with Grilled Vegetables

Grilled vegetables add a flavorful touch to a creamy risotto.

1 medium yellow onion, cut into ½-inch slices
1 zucchini, cut lengthwise into halves
Olive oil
1 *each* small red and yellow bell peppers
1 tablespoon butter
1 cup arborio rice

3 to 3½ cups canned chicken broth, divided
½ cup dry sherry
⅔ cup freshly grated Parmesan cheese
Black pepper
¼ cup toasted pine nuts
Chopped parsley

Insert wooden picks into onion slices from edges to prevent separating into rings. (Soak wooden picks in hot water 15 minutes to prevent burning.) Brush onion and zucchini lightly with oil. Grill onion, zucchini and bell peppers on covered grill over medium Kingsford briquets 5 to 10 minutes for zucchini and 20 to 30 minutes for peppers and onion or until crisp-tender. Cut vegetables into chunks. Heat butter and 1 tablespoon oil in 3-quart saucepan over medium heat. Add rice; cook and stir 3 to 4 minutes or until opaque. Add ¼ cup broth and sherry; cook 3 to 5 minutes over medium-low heat until almost all liquid is absorbed, stirring constantly. Continue adding broth in about ¾-cup increments, cooking and stirring after each addition until broth is absorbed and rice is tender and creamy. Stir in Parmesan cheese with last addition of broth. Season to taste with black pepper; stir in pine nuts and grilled vegetables, reserving a few for garnish. Spoon risotto into serving dish; top with reserved vegetables and parsley.

Makes 6 to 8 servings

Nutrients per Serving (⅛ of recipe): Calories: 233, protein: 8 g, fat: 12 g, carbohydrate: 25 g, sodium: 440 mg, cholesterol: 9 mg

Fresh Grilled Corn Soup

Grilled Corn (recipe follows)
Grilled Onion (recipe
  follows)
2 medium potatoes, peeled
  and cubed
1 can (49½ ounces) chicken
  broth (about 6 cups)

½ teaspoon ground cumin
½ teaspoon chili powder
1½ cups heavy cream or
  half-and-half
Chopped fresh cilantro
½ teaspoon hot pepper sauce

Prepare Grilled Corn and Grilled Onion. Cut corn from cobs. Chop onion.
Combine corn, onion, potatoes, broth, cumin and chili powder in Dutch
oven. Bring to a boil. Reduce heat to medium-low; simmer about
30 minutes until potatoes are tender. Place in food processor in batches.
Process until no large pieces remain, but mixture is not completely
smooth. Return to Dutch oven; stir in cream, ⅓ cup cilantro and pepper
sauce. Heat over low heat until warm. *Do not boil.* Ladle into bowls.
Garnish with additional cilantro.   *Makes 8 servings (1 cup each)*

Grilled Corn: Pull back husks from 4 ears of corn, leaving husks attached.
Remove 1 strip of husk from inner portion of each ear and reserve; remove
silk. Combine 1½ tablespoons melted butter, ½ teaspoon ground cumin,
¼ teaspoon chili powder and 1 teaspoon chopped fresh cilantro in small
bowl; brush onto corn. Bring husks up each ear to cover corn; secure with
reserved strips of husk. Grill on covered grill over medium Kingsford
briquets 20 to 30 minutes or until tender, turning once or twice.

Grilled Onion: Cut 1 medium onion into ½-inch-thick rounds. Insert
wooden picks into onion slices from edges to prevent separating into
rings. (Soak wooden picks in hot water 15 minutes to prevent burning.)
Brush onion slices with olive oil. Grill onion on covered grill over
medium Kingsford briquets 20 to 30 minutes or until tender, turning
once. Remove picks.

Nutrients per Serving: Calories: 199, protein: 7 g, fat: 10 g, carbohydrate: 22 g,
sodium: 697 mg, cholesterol: 23 mg

Fresh Grilled Corn Soup

Grilled Garlic

Grilling lends a sweet, mellow flavor to garlic, making it an
excellent addition to many dishes. Use it more generously than its
fresh counterpart. Whenever you grill, place a head or two of garlic
at the edge of the coals and grill alongside the main event.

1 or 2 heads garlic   **Olive oil**

Peel outermost papery skin from garlic heads. Brush heads with oil. Grill
heads at edge of grid on covered grill over medium-hot Kingsford briquets
30 to 45 minutes or until cloves are soft and buttery. Remove from grill;
cool slightly. Gently squeeze softened garlic head from root end so that
cloves slip out of skins into small bowl. Use immediately or cover and
refrigerate up to 1 week.

Serving Suggestions

• For a quick appetizer, spread cloves of Grilled Garlic over toasted bread
slices, crackers or raw vegetable slices.

• Mash cloves of Grilled Garlic and add to baked potatoes, mashed
potatoes, pasta dishes, soups, salad dressings and dips.

• Spread cloves of Grilled Garlic over bread slices for a flavorful, low-fat
sandwich spread. Or, mash cloves and add to mayonnaise.

• Spread cloves of Grilled Garlic onto a pizza crust before adding
toppings.

• To season steamed vegetables, mash cloves of Grilled Garlic and stir into
melted or softened butter with chopped fresh herbs or spices.

Grilled Greek Vegetables

¼ cup olive oil
1 tablespoon lemon juice
2 teaspoons pressed garlic
1 teaspoon dried oregano
  leaves

1 pound assorted fresh
  vegetables, such as
  eggplant, bell peppers,
  summer squash,
  mushrooms and onions

Combine oil, lemon juice, garlic and oregano in large bowl. Slice eggplant into ½-inch-thick rounds.* Cut small squash lengthwise into halves; cut large squash into ½-inch-thick pieces. Cut bell peppers into large chunks. Cut onions into wedges or thick slices. Toss vegetables with oil mixture to coat. Place vegetables in single layer on grid; reserve remaining oil mixture. Grill on covered grill over medium Kingsford briquets 10 to 20 minutes or until tender, turning once and basting with remaining oil mixture. *Makes 4 servings*

If desired, eggplant slices can be salted on both sides and placed in single layer on paper towels. Let stand 30 minutes; blot dry with paper towels.

Nutrients per Serving: Calories: 155, protein: 2 g, fat: 14 g, carbohydrate: 8 g, sodium: 4 mg, cholesterol: 0 mg

Stuffed Portobello Mushrooms

A dense, meaty texture makes portobello mushrooms ideal for stuffing and grilling. Serve them as an hors d'oeuvre or first course.

4 portobello mushrooms (4 ounces each)
¼ cup olive oil
2 cloves garlic, pressed
6 ounces crumbled goat cheese

2 ounces prosciutto or thinly sliced ham, chopped
¼ cup chopped fresh basil
Mixed salad greens

Remove stems and gently scrape gills from underside of mushrooms; discard stems and gills. Brush mushroom caps with combined oil and garlic. Combine cheese, prosciutto and basil in medium bowl. Grill mushrooms, top side up, on covered grill over medium Kingsford briquets 4 minutes. Turn mushrooms over; fill caps with cheese mixture, dividing equally. Cover and grill 3 to 4 minutes longer until cheese mixture is warm. Remove mushrooms from grill; cut into quarters. Serve on mixed greens. *Makes 4 servings*

Nutrients per Serving: Calories: 298, protein: 13 g, fat: 25 g, carbohydrate: 8 g, sodium: 353 mg, cholesterol: 28 mg

Salmon, Asparagus and Shiitake Salad

¼ cup cider vinegar

¼ cup extra-virgin olive oil

Grated peel and juice of
  1 lemon

4 teaspoons Dijon mustard,
  divided

1 clove garlic, minced

¼ teaspoon salt

¼ teaspoon black pepper

2 teaspoons minced fresh
  tarragon *or* ¾ teaspoon
  dried tarragon leaves

1 pound small salmon fillets,
  skinned

1 medium red onion, thinly
  sliced

1 pound asparagus, ends
  trimmed

¼ pound shiitake mushrooms
  or button mushrooms

Additional salt and black
  pepper

8 cups lightly packed torn
  romaine and red leaf
  lettuce

Combine vinegar, oil, juice, peel, 2 teaspoons mustard, garlic, ¼ teaspoon salt and ¼ teaspoon pepper in medium bowl; spoon 3 tablespoons dressing into 2-quart glass dish to use as marinade. Reserve remaining dressing. Add tarragon and 2 teaspoons remaining mustard to marinade in glass dish; blend well. Add salmon; turn to coat. Cover and refrigerate 1 hour. Transfer 3 tablespoons of reserved dressing to medium bowl; add onion, tossing to coat. Thread asparagus and mushrooms onto wooden skewers. (Soak skewers in hot water 30 minutes to prevent burning.)

Remove salmon from marinade; discard marinade. Season salmon to taste with additional salt and pepper. Lightly oil hot grid to prevent sticking. Grill salmon over medium-hot Kingsford briquets 2 to 4 minutes per side until fish flakes when tested with fork. Grill asparagus and mushrooms over medium-hot briquets 5 to 8 minutes until crisp-tender. Cut asparagus into 2-inch pieces and slice mushrooms; add to onion mixture. Let stand 10 minutes. Toss lettuce with onion mixture in large bowl; arrange lettuce on platter. Break salmon into 2-inch pieces; arrange salmon and vegetables over lettuce. Drizzle with remaining reserved dressing. Serve immediately.

Makes 4 main-dish servings

Nutrients per Serving: Calories: 282, protein: 24 g, fat: 16 g, carbohydrate: 13 g, sodium: 127 mg, cholesterol: 55 mg

Salmon, Asparagus and Shiitake Salad

Goat Cheese & Corn Chiles Rellenos

4 large plum tomatoes, seeded and diced

1 small red onion, diced and divided

3 tablespoons extra-virgin olive oil, divided

2 cloves garlic, minced and divided

1 teaspoon balsamic vinegar

¼ teaspoon salt

¼ teaspoon black pepper

6 poblano *or* 8 Anaheim peppers

2 ears corn, husked*

¾ cup crumbled goat or feta cheese

½ cup (2 ounces) shredded hot pepper Jack, Monterey Jack or sharp Cheddar cheese

½ cup minced fresh cilantro

Fresh cilantro sprigs

Combine tomatoes, ½ onion, 2 tablespoons oil, 1 clove garlic, vinegar, salt and black pepper in medium bowl; let salsa stand 15 minutes. Remove stems from poblano peppers by cutting each pepper about ½ inch from stem; remove seeds. Grill peppers over medium-hot Kingsford briquets until skins are charred on all sides. Place peppers in large resealable plastic food storage bag; seal. Let stand 5 minutes; remove skin. Grill corn over medium-hot briquets 6 to 10 minutes or until tender, turning every minute; cut kernels from cob. Combine corn, cheeses, minced cilantro, remaining ½ onion and 1 clove garlic in medium bowl; mix well. Carefully fill each pepper with cheese mixture, making cut in side of pepper, if necessary. Secure opening with wooden pick. (Soak wooden picks in hot water 15 minutes to prevent burning.) Brush peppers with remaining 1 tablespoon oil; grill over medium briquets 1 minute per side until cheese melts. Serve with salsa. Garnish with cilantro sprigs.

Makes 6 servings

Substitute 1 can (17 ounces) corn, drained, or 1½ cups frozen corn, thawed, for fresh corn, if desired. Add to filling as directed above.

Nutrients per Serving: Calories: 209, protein: 7 g, fat: 13 g, carbohydrate: 16 g, sodium: 234 mg, cholesterol: 18 mg

Goat Cheese & Corn Chile Relleno

Pizzas, Sandwiches & More

Grilled Chile Chicken Quesadillas

2 tablespoons lime juice
3 cloves garlic, minced
1 tablespoon ground cumin
1 tablespoon chili powder
1 tablespoon vegetable oil
1 jalapeño pepper, minced
1 teaspoon salt
6 skinless boneless chicken
   thighs

3 poblano peppers, cut in half,
   stemmed, seeded
2 avocados, peeled and sliced
3 cups (12 ounces) shredded
   Monterey Jack cheese
12 (8-inch) flour tortillas
1½ cups fresh salsa
   Red chiles
   Fresh cilantro sprigs

Combine lime juice, garlic, cumin, chili powder, oil, jalapeño pepper and
salt in small bowl; coat chicken with paste. Cover and refrigerate chicken
at least 15 minutes. Grill chicken on covered grill over medium-hot
Kingsford briquets 4 minutes per side until no longer pink in center.
Grill poblano peppers, skin side down, 8 minutes until skins are charred.
Place peppers in large resealable plastic food storage bag; seal. Let stand
5 minutes; remove skin. Cut chicken and peppers into strips. Arrange
chicken, peppers, avocado and cheese on half of each tortilla. Drizzle with
2 tablespoons salsa. Fold other half of tortilla over filling. Grill quesadillas
on covered grill over medium briquets 30 seconds to 1 minute per side
until cheese is melted. Garnish with chiles and cilantro sprigs.

Makes 12 quesadillas

Nutrients per Serving (1 quesadilla): Calories: 363, protein: 18 g, fat: 18 g, carbohydrate: 26 g,
sodium: 695 mg, cholesterol: 58 mg

Grilled Chile Chicken Quesadillas

Magic Carpet Kabobs

Marinate chicken thighs overnight in a marinade reminiscent of the exotic flavors of the cuisines of far-off lands.

1 cup orange juice
½ cup bottled mango chutney, divided
2 tablespoons lemon juice
1 tablespoon grated fresh ginger
2 cloves garlic, pressed
2 teaspoons ground cumin
1 teaspoon grated lemon peel
1 teaspoon grated orange peel
1 teaspoon red pepper flakes
¼ teaspoon salt
4 skinless boneless chicken thighs, cut into chunks
1 medium yellow onion, cut into chunks
4 whole pita bread rounds
½ cup plain low-fat yogurt
¾ cup chopped cucumber
Orange peel strips

Combine orange juice, ¼ cup chutney, lemon juice, ginger, garlic, cumin, grated peels, pepper and salt, blending well; reserve ¼ cup marinade for basting. Combine remaining marinade and chicken in large resealable plastic food storage bag. Seal bag; turn to coat evenly. Marinate in refrigerator overnight. Thread chicken alternately with onion onto 4 long wooden skewers, dividing equally. (Soak wooden skewers in hot water 30 minutes to prevent burning.) Lightly oil grid to prevent sticking. Grill kabobs over medium-hot Kingsford briquets 10 to 12 minutes until chicken is no longer pink, turning once and basting with reserved marinade. Grill pita breads 1 or 2 minutes until warm. Combine yogurt and remaining ¼ cup chutney. Spoon yogurt mixture down centers of pitas; top with cucumber, dividing equally. Top each with kabob; remove skewer. Garnish with orange peel strips. *Makes 4 servings*

Nutrients per Serving: Calories: 282, protein: 24 g, fat: 17 g, carbohydrate: 8 g, sodium: 676 mg, cholesterol: 70 mg

Magic Carpet Kabob

Pesto Chicken & Pepper Wraps

Purchased pesto sauce is the secret to these quick and delicious wraps. It flavors the marinade and then it is spread on the tortillas.

⅔ cup refrigerated pesto sauce or frozen pesto sauce, thawed and divided
3 tablespoons red wine vinegar
¼ teaspoon salt
¼ teaspoon black pepper
1¼ pounds skinless boneless chicken thighs or breasts
2 red bell peppers, cut in half, stemmed and seeded

5 (8-inch) flour tortillas
5 thin slices (3-inch rounds) fresh-pack mozzarella cheese*
5 leaves Boston or red leaf lettuce
Orange slices
Red and green chiles
Fresh basil sprigs

Combine ¼ cup pesto, vinegar, salt and black pepper in medium bowl. Add chicken; toss to coat. Cover and refrigerate at least 30 minutes. Remove chicken from marinade; discard marinade. Grill chicken over medium-hot Kingsford briquets about 4 minutes per side until chicken is no longer pink in center, turning once. Grill bell peppers, skin sides down, about 8 minutes until skin is charred. Place bell peppers in large resealable plastic food storage bag; seal. Let stand 5 minutes; remove skin. Cut chicken and bell peppers into thin strips. Spread about 1 tablespoon of remaining pesto down center of each tortilla; top with chicken, bell peppers, cheese and lettuce. Roll tortillas to enclose filling. Garnish with orange slices, chiles and basil sprigs. *Makes 5 wraps*

*Packaged sliced whole milk or part-skim mozzarella cheese can be substituted for fresh-pack mozzarella cheese.

Nutrients per Serving (1 wrap): Calories: 481, protein: 40 g, fat: 24 g, carbohydrate: 26 g, sodium: 596 mg, cholesterol: 106 mg

Pesto Chicken & Pepper Wrap

Caramelized Onion & Eggplant Sandwiches

Eggplant and onion soak up the flavors of Southeast Asian cuisines in this vegetarian sandwich.

Grilled Garlic Aioli (recipe
  follows) or mayonnaise
½ cup packed brown sugar
½ cup water
½ cup soy sauce
2 tablespoons molasses
5 slices fresh ginger
¼ teaspoon ground coriander
  Dash black pepper

1 large yellow onion
4 large eggplant slices,
  1 inch thick
4 round buns, split
4 tomato slices
  Mixed greens
  Radishes
  Carrot curls

Prepare Grilled Garlic Aioli; set aside. Combine sugar, water, soy sauce, molasses, ginger, coriander and pepper in small saucepan. Bring to boil, stirring constantly. Reduce heat; simmer marinade 5 minutes, stirring occasionally. Cool. Cut onion into ½-inch-thick slices. Insert wooden picks into onion slices from edges to prevent separating into rings. (Soak wooden picks in hot water 15 minutes to prevent burning.) Marinate eggplant and onion in marinade 10 to 15 minutes. Remove vegetables from marinade; reserve marinade. Lightly oil grid to prevent sticking. Grill vegetables on covered grill around edge of medium-hot Kingsford briquets about 20 minutes or until tender, turning once or twice and brushing with reserved marinade. Place buns on grill, cut sides down, until toasted. Serve eggplant and onion on grilled buns with tomato, greens and Grilled Garlic Aioli. Garnish with radishes and carrot curls.

Makes 4 sandwiches

Grilled Garlic Aioli: Prepare Grilled Garlic (page 72). Mash 8 cloves Grilled Garlic in small bowl. Add ¼ cup mayonnaise; mix until blended.

Nutrients per Serving: Calories: 334, protein: 7 g, fat: 15 g, carbohydrate: 46 g, sodium: 414 mg, cholesterol: 21 mg

Caramelized Onion &
Eggplant Sandwich

Vietnamese Grilled Steak Wraps

Each bite teases the taste buds with the flavors of fresh mint, cilantro, tangy lemon and fiery chile sauce. Heavenly!

1 beef flank steak (about
   1½ pounds)
Grated peel and juice of
   2 lemons
6 tablespoons sugar, divided
2 tablespoons dark sesame oil
1¼ teaspoons salt, divided
½ teaspoon black pepper
¼ cup water
¼ cup rice vinegar

½ teaspoon crushed red pepper
6 (8-inch) flour tortillas
6 red leaf lettuce leaves
⅓ cup lightly packed fresh
   mint leaves
⅓ cup lightly packed fresh
   cilantro leaves
Star fruit slices
Red bell pepper strips
Orange peel strips

Cut beef across the grain into thin slices. Combine lemon peel, juice, 2 tablespoons sugar, sesame oil, 1 teaspoon salt and black pepper in medium bowl. Add beef; toss to coat. Cover and refrigerate at least 30 minutes. Combine water, vinegar, remaining 4 tablespoons sugar and ¼ teaspoon salt in small saucepan; bring to a boil. Boil 5 minutes without stirring until syrupy. Stir in crushed red pepper; set aside.

Remove beef from marinade; discard marinade. Thread beef onto metal or wooden skewers. (Soak wooden skewers in hot water 30 minutes to prevent burning.) Grill beef over medium-hot Kingsford briquets about 3 minutes per side until cooked through. Grill tortillas until hot. Place lettuce, beef, mint and cilantro on tortillas; drizzle with vinegar mixture. Roll tortillas to enclose filling. Garnish with star fruit, bell pepper and orange peel strips.

Makes 6 wraps

Nutrients per Serving (1 wrap): Calories: 366, protein: 25 g, fat: 16 g, carbohydrate: 28 g, sodium: 340 mg, cholesterol: 61 mg

Vietnamese Grilled Steak Wrap

Grilled Garlic & Herb Pizzas

Homemade Pizza Dough
(page 90)
8 cloves Grilled Garlic
(page 72)
1 medium yellow onion
Olive oil
1 medium red, yellow or
orange bell pepper

1 cup crumbled goat cheese
¼ cup chopped fresh herb
mixture (thyme, basil,
oregano and parsley) *or*
4 teaspoons dry herb
mixture
¼ cup grated Parmesan cheese

Prepare Homemade Pizza Dough. While dough is rising, light Kingsford briquets in covered grill. Arrange medium-hot briquets on one side of the grill. Prepare Grilled Garlic. Lightly oil grid to prevent sticking. Cut onion into ½-inch-thick slices. Insert wooden picks into onion slices from edges to prevent separating into rings. (Soak wooden picks in hot water 15 minutes to prevent burning.) Brush onion lightly with oil. Place whole bell pepper and onion slices on grid around edge of briquets. Grill on covered grill 20 to 30 minutes until tender, turning once or twice. Remove picks from onion slices and separate into rings. Cut pepper in half and remove seeds; slice pepper halves into strips.

Roll or gently stretch each ball of dough into 7-inch round. Brush lightly with oil on both sides. Grill dough on grid directly above medium-hot Kingsford briquets 1 to 3 minutes or until dough starts to bubble and bottom is lightly browned. Turn; grill 3 to 5 minutes or until second side is lightly browned and dough is cooked through. Remove from grill. Spread 2 cloves Grilled Garlic onto each crust; top with onion, pepper, goat cheese, herbs and Parmesan cheese, dividing equally. Place pizzas around edge of coals; grill covered 5 minutes until bottom crust is crisp, cheese melts and toppings are heated through.

Makes 4 individual pizzas

Note: A 1-pound loaf of frozen bread dough, thawed, can be substituted for Homemade Pizza Dough. Or, substitute 4 pre-baked individual Italian bread shells, add toppings and warm on the grill.

continued on page 90

Grilled Garlic & Herb Pizzas

Grilled Garlic & Herb Pizzas, continued

Homemade Pizza Dough

2¾ cups all-purpose flour, divided

1 package quick-rising yeast

¾ teaspoon salt

1 cup water

1½ tablespoons vegetable oil

Combine 1½ cups flour, yeast and salt in food processor. Heat water and oil in small saucepan until 120° to 130°F. With food processor running, add water and oil to flour mixture; process 30 seconds. Add 1 cup flour; process until dough comes together to form ball. Knead on floured board 3 to 4 minutes or until smooth and satiny, kneading in as much of the remaining ¼ cup flour as needed to prevent dough from sticking. Place dough in oiled bowl, turning once. Cover with towel; let rise in warm place 30 minutes until doubled in bulk. Divide dough into 4 equal balls.

Nutrients per Serving (1 individual pizza): Calories: 533, protein: 19 g, fat: 21 g, carbohydrate: 68 g, sodium: 668 mg, cholesterol: 20 mg

Cajun Catfish Sandwiches

Make an extra batch of seasoning mix to keep on hand.

Aioli Tartar Sauce (page 91)

4½ teaspoons paprika

1 tablespoon dried oregano leaves

1½ teaspoons salt

¾ teaspoon granulated garlic

½ teaspoon white pepper

½ teaspoon black pepper

½ teaspoon cayenne pepper

4 small catfish fillets (1¼ pounds)

Lemon juice

4 sourdough rolls, split

4 cups finely shredded cabbage

Lemon wedges

Prepare Aioli Tartar Sauce; set aside. Combine paprika, oregano, salt, garlic and peppers until blended. Brush catfish with lemon juice; sprinkle evenly with seasoning mix to coat. Lightly oil grid to prevent sticking. Grill over medium-hot Kingsford briquets, allowing 10 minutes cooking time for each inch of thickness, turning once. Spread Aioli Tartar Sauce onto insides of rolls. Top each roll with catfish fillet and 1 cup cabbage. Serve with lemon wedges. *Makes 4 sandwiches*

Aioli Tartar Sauce: Prepare Grilled Garlic (page 72). Combine ½ cup mayonnaise, 12 mashed cloves Grilled Garlic, 2 teaspoons *each* lemon juice and chopped parsley, and 1 teaspoon chopped, drained capers; blend well.

Nutrients per Serving: Calories: 508, protein: 33 g, fat: 30 g, carbohydrate: 29 g, sodium: 1296 mg, cholesterol: 98 mg

Turkey Picatta on Grilled Rolls

¼ **cup lemon juice**
¼ **cup olive oil**
2 **tablespoons capers in liquid, chopped**
2 **cloves garlic, pressed**
  Black pepper
1 **pound turkey breast slices**
4 **soft French rolls, cut into halves**

4 **thin slices mozzarella or Swiss cheese (optional)**
  Lettuce (optional)
  Red bell pepper slivers (optional)
  Additional capers (optional)

Combine lemon juice, oil, 2 tablespoons capers with liquid, garlic and black pepper to taste in shallow glass dish or large resealable plastic food storage bag. Add turkey; turn to coat. Cover and marinate in refrigerator several hours or overnight. Remove turkey from marinade; discard marinade. Lightly oil grid to help prevent sticking. Grill turkey over medium-hot Kingsford briquets 2 minutes until turkey is no longer pink, turning once. Move cooked turkey slices to edge of grill to keep warm. Grill rolls, cut sides down, until toasted. Fill rolls with hot turkey slices, dividing equally. Add cheese, lettuce, bell pepper and additional capers, if desired. *Makes 4 servings*

Nutrients per Serving: Calories: 295, protein: 31 g, fat: 3 g, carbohydrate: 31 g, sodium: 374 mg, cholesterol: 73 mg

Barbecue Pizzas

Homemade Pizza Dough
(page 90)
1 medium yellow onion
Olive oil
½ cup plus 2 tablespoons
K.C. Masterpiece Original
Barbecue Sauce, divided

6 ounces thinly sliced grilled
pork or chicken
2 cups (8 ounces) shredded
smoked Gouda or
mozzarella cheese
¼ cup chopped fresh cilantro

Prepare Homemade Pizza Dough. While dough is rising, light Kingsford briquets in grill. Arrange medium-hot briquets on one side of grill. Lightly oil grid to prevent sticking. Slice onion into ½-inch-thick slices. Insert wooden picks into onion slices from edges to prevent separating into rings. (Soak wooden picks in hot water 15 minutes to prevent burning.) Brush onion lightly with oil. Place on grid around edge of briquets. Grill onion on covered grill 20 to 30 minutes or until tender. Brush with 2 tablespoons barbecue sauce during last 5 minutes of grilling. Remove picks and separate onion into rings; set aside.

Roll or gently stretch each ball of dough into 7-inch round. Brush lightly with oil on both sides. Grill dough on grid directly above medium-hot Kingsford briquets 1 to 3 minutes or until dough starts to bubble and bottom is lightly browned. Turn; grill 3 to 5 minutes or until second side is lightly browned and dough is cooked through. Remove from grill. Brush crusts with remaining ½ cup barbecue sauce; top with grilled pork, onion rings, cheese and cilantro, dividing equally. Place pizzas around edge of briquets; grill covered about 5 minutes until bottom crust is crisp, cheese melts and toppings are heated through.   *Makes 4 individual pizzas*

Note: A 1-pound loaf of frozen bread dough, thawed, can be substituted for Homemade Pizza Dough. Or, substitute pre-baked individual Italian bread shells. Add toppings and warm on grill.

Nutrients per Serving: Calories: 688, protein: 35 g, fat: 29 g, carbohydrate: 70 g, sodium: 1035 mg, cholesterol: 88 mg

Index